Ferdinando Carulli Guitar Concertos

E Minor, Op. 140
A Major, Op. 8A

PLAYBACK+
Speed • Pitch • Balance • Loop

To access audio visit:
www.halleonard.com/mylibrary

Enter Code
4153-5305-1954-1243

ISBN 978-1-59615-761-3

Music Minus One

EXCLUSIVELY DISTRIBUTED BY

HAL•LEONARD®

Visit Hal Leonard Online at
www.halleonard.com

Contact us:
Hal Leonard
7777 West Bluemound Road
Milwaukee, WI 53213
Email: info@halleonard.com

In Europe, contact:
Hal Leonard Europe Limited
42 Wigmore Street
Marylebone, London, W1U 2RN
Email: info@halleonardeurope.com

In Australia, contact:
Hal Leonard Australia Pty. Ltd.
4 Lentara Court
Cheltenham, Victoria, 3192 Australia
Email: info@halleonard.com.au

PERFORMANCE NOTES

THESE PRESENT GUITAR CONCERTI are, like the Vivaldi Concerti (HL0040067), a very good introduction for young guitarists to the literature for guitar and orchestra.

Although at first sight they look quite easy to play, one feels that it is a lot of work when studying them and attempting to play them on a professional level. They have to sound very clear and understandable, also in a very classical style and form. For me it was very helpful to listen to some good piano interpreters playing Mozart piano concerti, and at the same time to study Carulli's other works for solo guitar to get into his style and intentions.

The trills in both concerti I mostly play over two strings, avoiding the hammer-on and pull-off technique on one string. The two notes then will sound one into the other, but the sound result in the end is much stronger.

—*Christian Reichert*
Lörrach (Germany)

Christian Reichert

Christian Reichert shows a command of the guitar that encompasses both extreme sensitivity and virtuosity. The guitarist with "the fascinating technical experience and perfect rhythm" won several international prizes in Spain (Andrés Segovia International Guitar Competition), Poland, Bulgaria (International Guitar Foundation) and Germany. Since then the artist who "fills the audience easily with enthusiasm" (*El País*, Spain) concertizes and gives master-classes frequently in the U.S. and other international venues, including Paris, Moscow, Granada, Montreux, Stockholm, Cracow, Sofia and Vienna.

Born in Würzburg, Germany, in 1971, he studied with Hans Koch and Johannes Tappert and at the Freiburg and Cologne academies with Sonja Prunnbauer and Argentinian master Roberto Aussel. During his studies he took part in master-classes with such guitarists as Leo Brouwer, Manuel Barrueco, Roland Dyens, Sharon Isbin, Alvaro Pierri, Hubert Käppel and others. His interest in chamber music gave him the opportunity to play in a master-class with the great singer Dietrich Fischer-Dieskau in Berlin. By age 21 he was a prize-winner at the Andres Segovia International Guitar Competition in Granada, Spain. He won several prizes at the international competitions in Krynica, Cracow, Poland, and Frechen, Germany; and received a scholarship from the Richard Wagner Foundation in Bayreuth. In 1998 he received First Prize at the International Guitar Foundation's competition in Plovdiv, Bulgaria, as well as First Prize at the 1999 International Competition for Contemporary Music in Frankfurt together with flautist Katarzyna Bury.

Mr. Reichert is a frequent teacher of master-classes and regularly performs as soloist and with all kinds of ensembles. Several composers have dedicated guitar works to him, and in addition to his much lauded and constantly broadening compact disc recordings for Music Minus One, he has recorded for many other labels and for many television and radio stations in Europe. In 2004 he began a CD-guitar series for Waterpipe Records in Germany. If you'd like to learn more about this extraordinary artist visit his website at *www.christianreichert.com*.

Nayden Todorov

One of the greatest of the younger generation of conductors working today, Nayden Todorov has forged a solid place for himself on the world stage, and has lent his experienced hand to many of Music Minus One's most exciting and successful releases. A native of Plovdiv, Bulgaria, Maestro Todorov conducted his first concert at age 16. He studied in Vienna under Karl Österreicher and Uros Lajovic, and has gone on to conduct major orchestras across the European continent, the U.S. and in Israel, where he was also resident conductor of the Haifa Symphony Orchestra. In 2000, Mr. Todorov became Music Director of both the Plovdiv Philharmonic Orchestra and of the Plovdiv National Opera. In 2003 he became Artistic Director of the Bourgas Philharmonic Orchestra. Currently he serves as as general manager and music director of the Rousse State Opera & Philharmonic and since the 2004/2005 season, has served as principal guest conductor of the Sofia National Philharmonic. In addition he is the Music Director of the much-lauded Thracia Summer International Music Festival.

In addition to his recordings for MMO, he has regularly recorded for Danacord, Naxos, and many other labels worldwide. He commands a vast range of symphonic, ballet and operatic repertoire and is one of the most in-demand conductors in the music world.

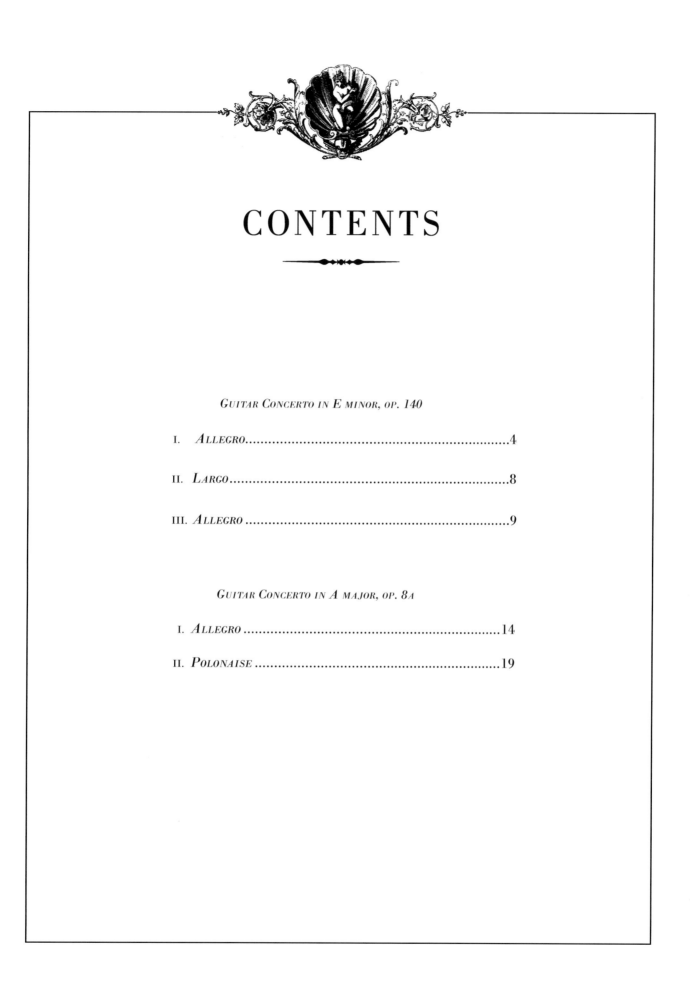

CONTENTS

Concerto in E Minor

For Guitar and Strings
"Petit Concerto"

Editing and fingering
by Christian Reichert

Ferdinando Carulli, Op. 140
(1770 - 1841)

* Because there is no orchestral accompaniment between measures 71 and 86, the accompaniment track of this movement is split. When performing with the accompaniment track, have a friend begin playing "Orchestra re-entry" at measure 86.

8

4 taps (1 measure) precede entry

Largo

Solo

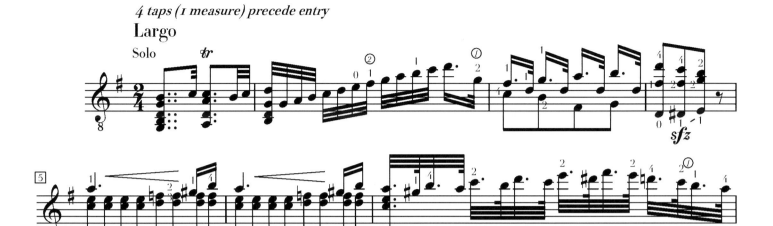

* Because there is no orchestral accompaniment until measure 9, the accompaniment track of this movement is split. When performing with the accompaniment track, have a friend begin playing "Orchestra re-entry" at measure 9.

Allegro

* Because there is no orchestral accompaniment between measures 53 and 68, the accompaniment track of this movement is split. When performing with the accompaniment track, have a friend begin playing "Orchestra re-entry" at measure 68.

Concerto in A major

For Guitar and Strings

*Editing and fingering
by Christian Reichert*

Ferdinando Carulli, op. 8a
(1770 - 1841)

CADENZA

* Because there is no orchestral accompaniment during the cadenza between measures 231 and 238, the accompaniment track of this movement is split. When performing with the accompaniment track, have a friend begin playing "Orchestra re-entry" near the end of the trill at measure 237.

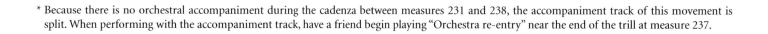

3 taps (1 measure) precede entry

Polonaise

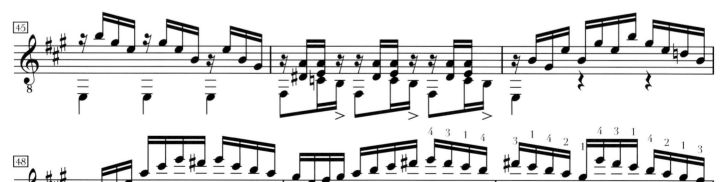

22

Minore

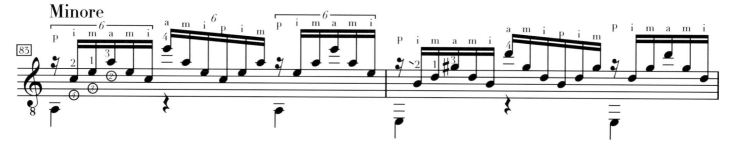

Engraving: Wieslaw Novak

MMO 3634

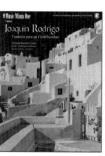